Zen Dragons

A Magical Coloring Book
Volume 1

by
Katherine Hacking

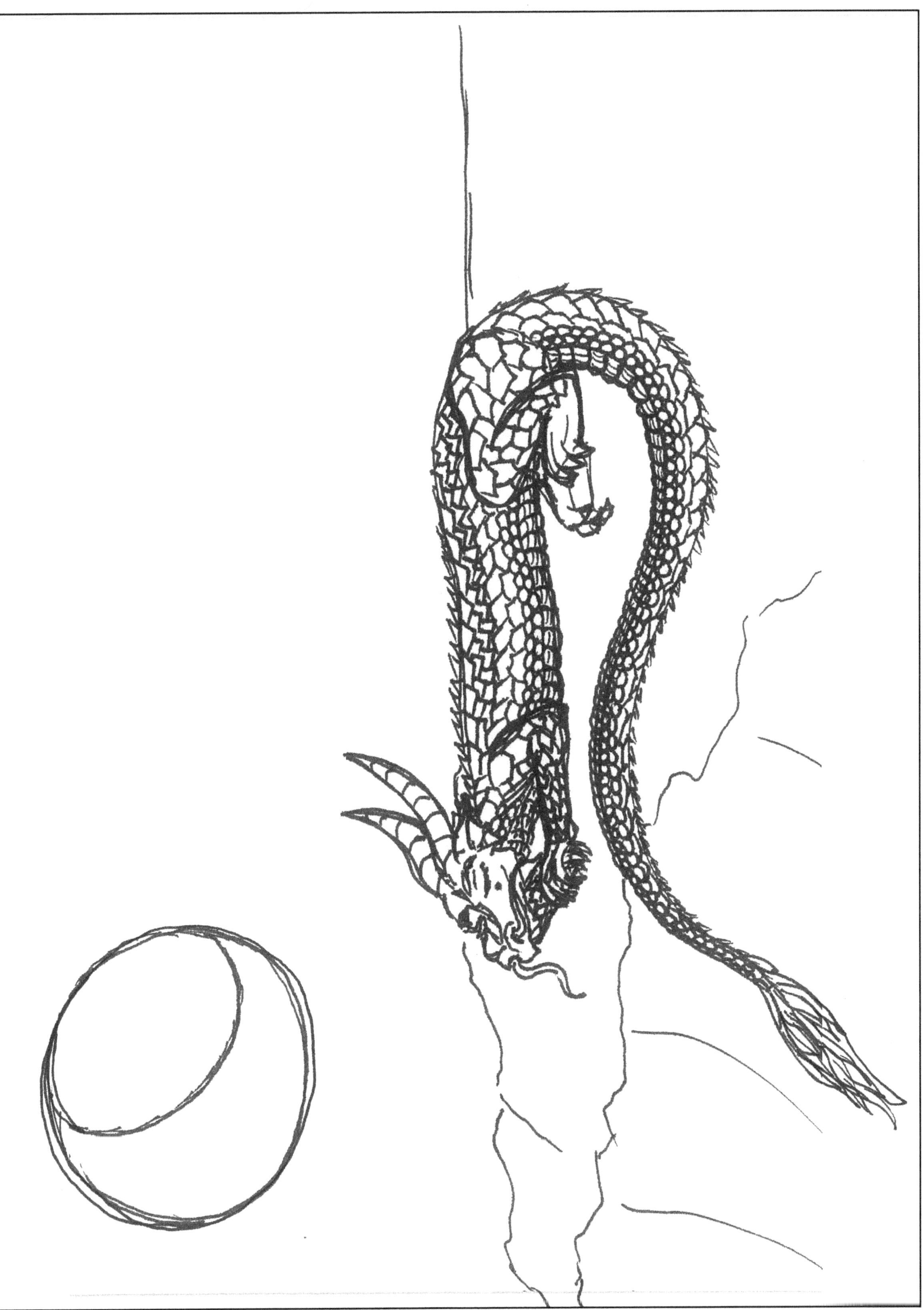

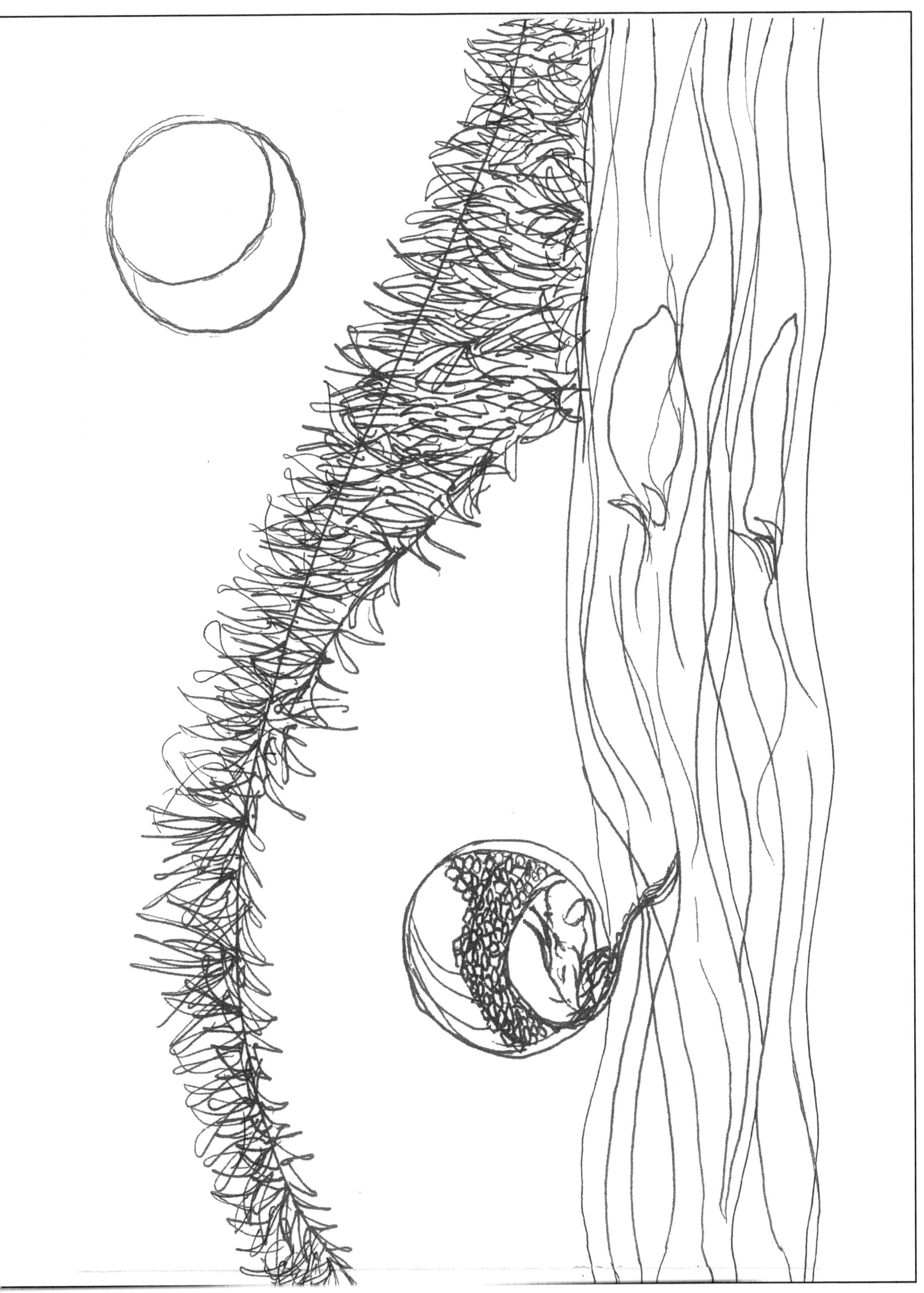

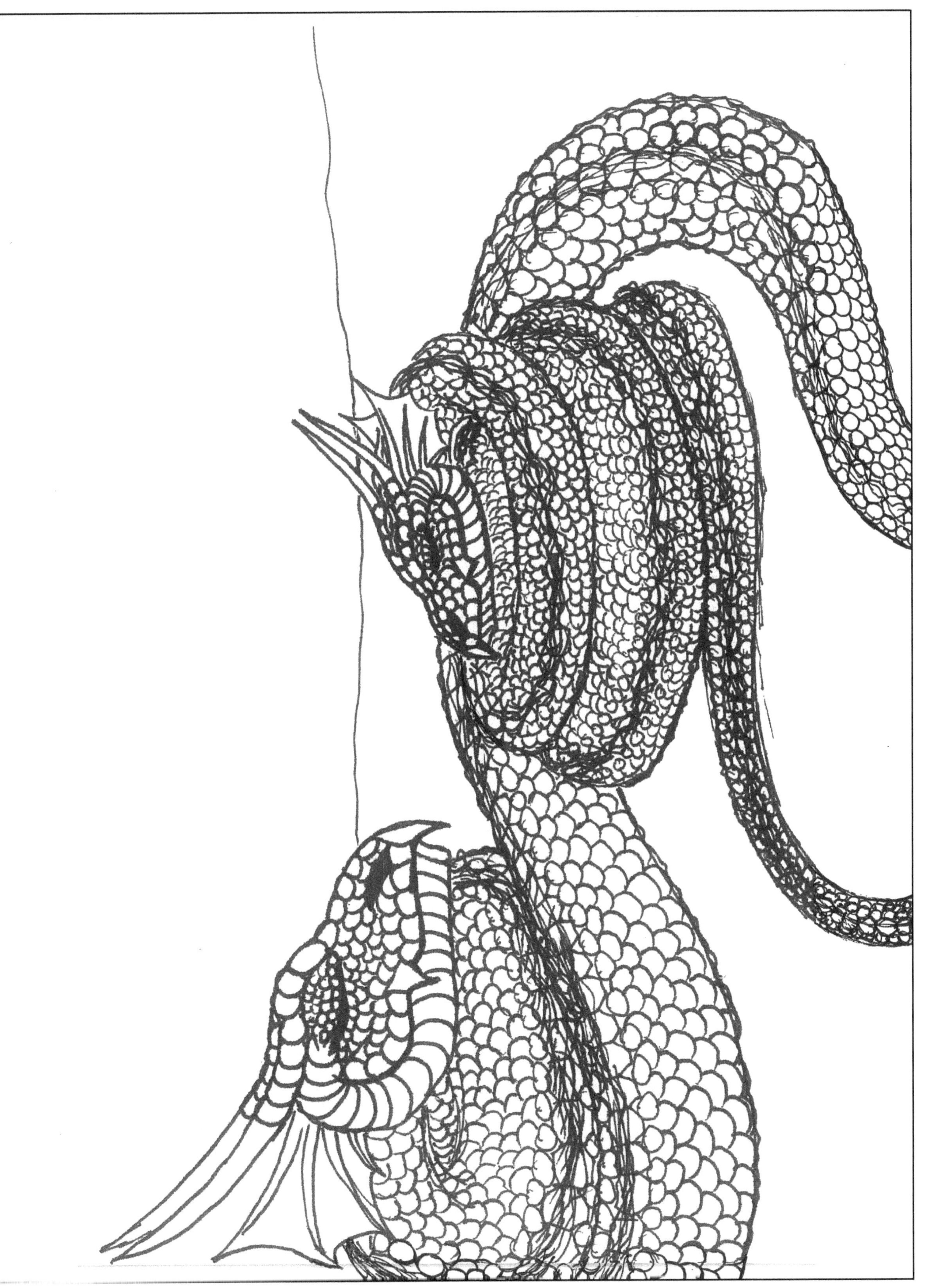

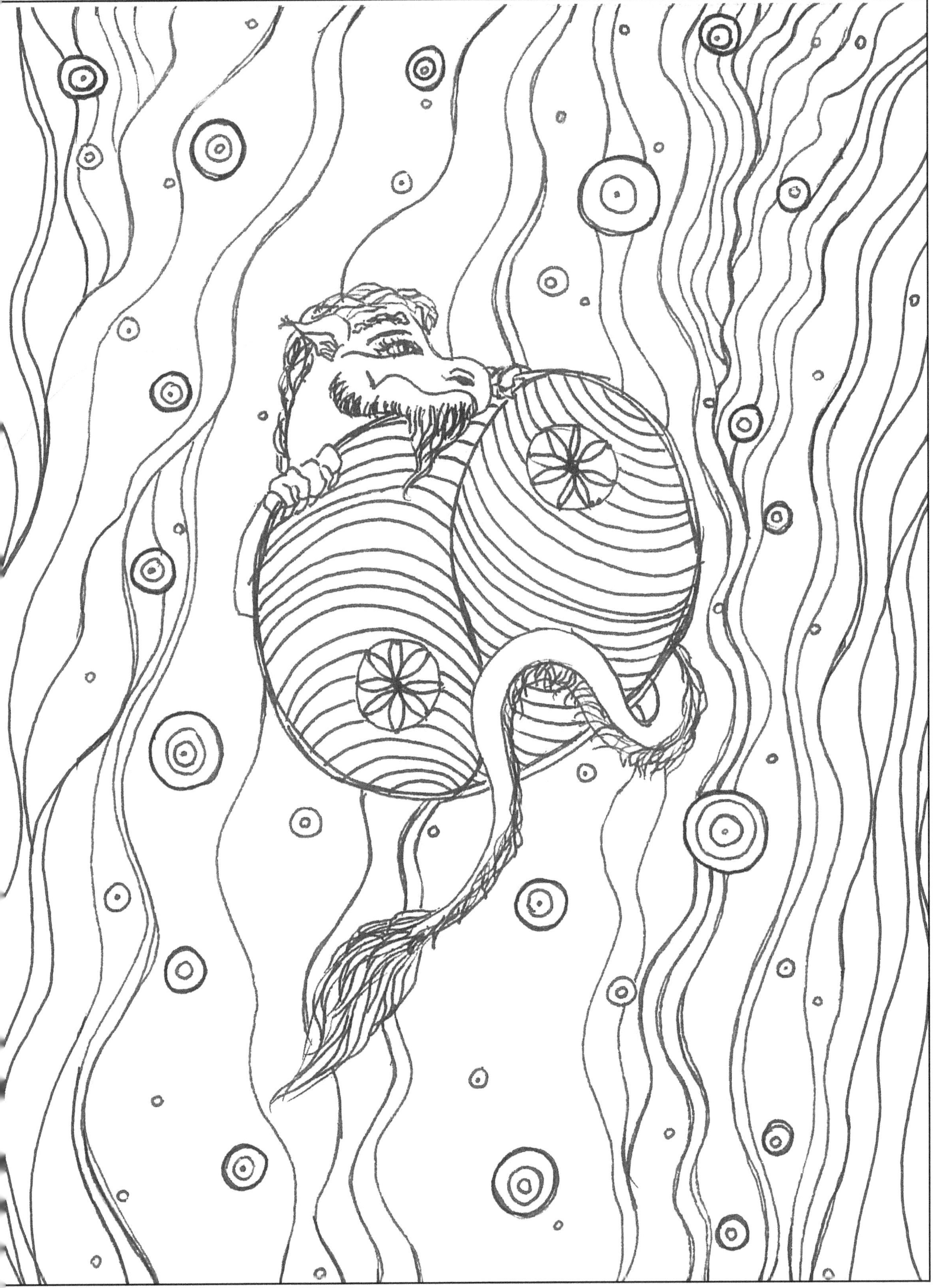

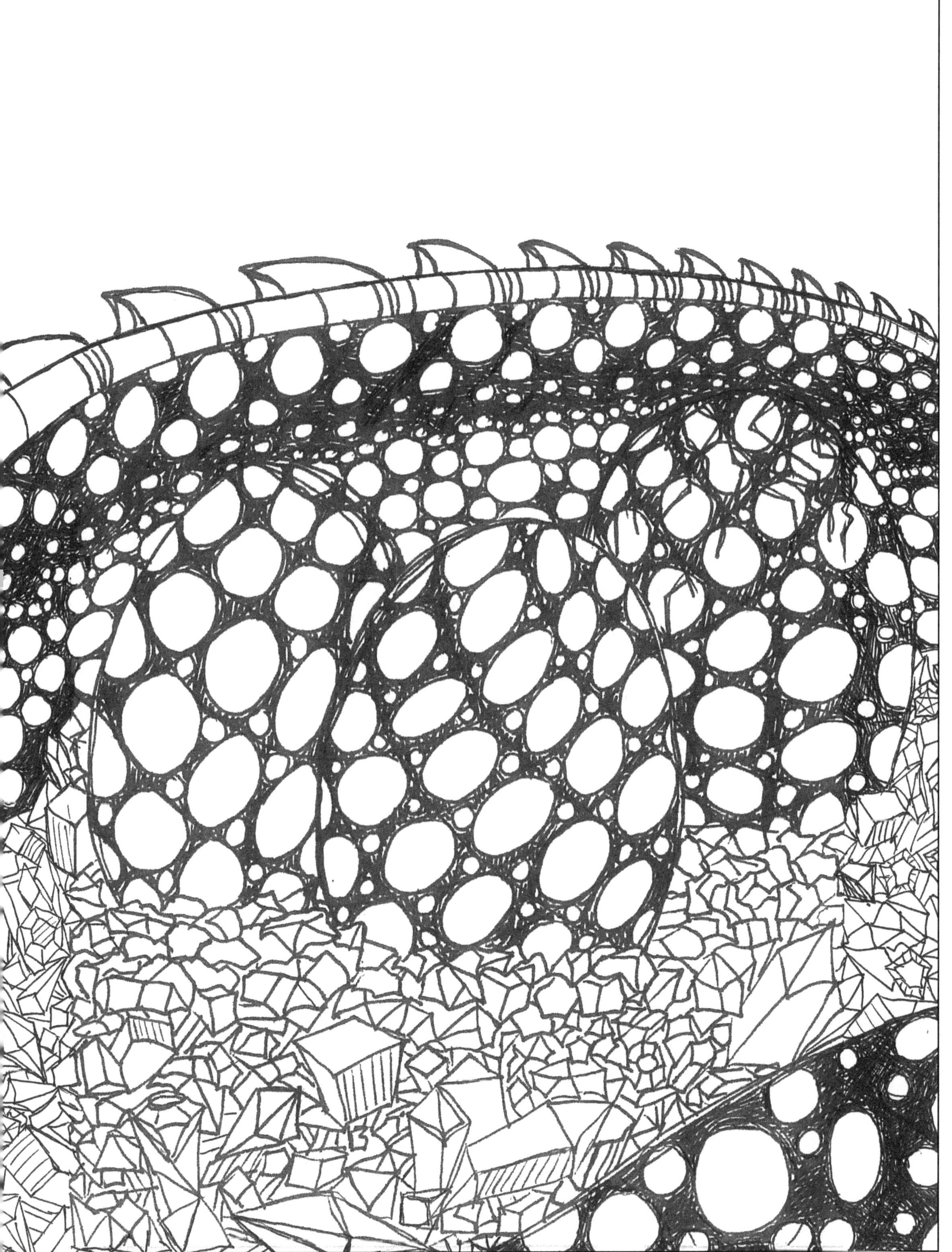

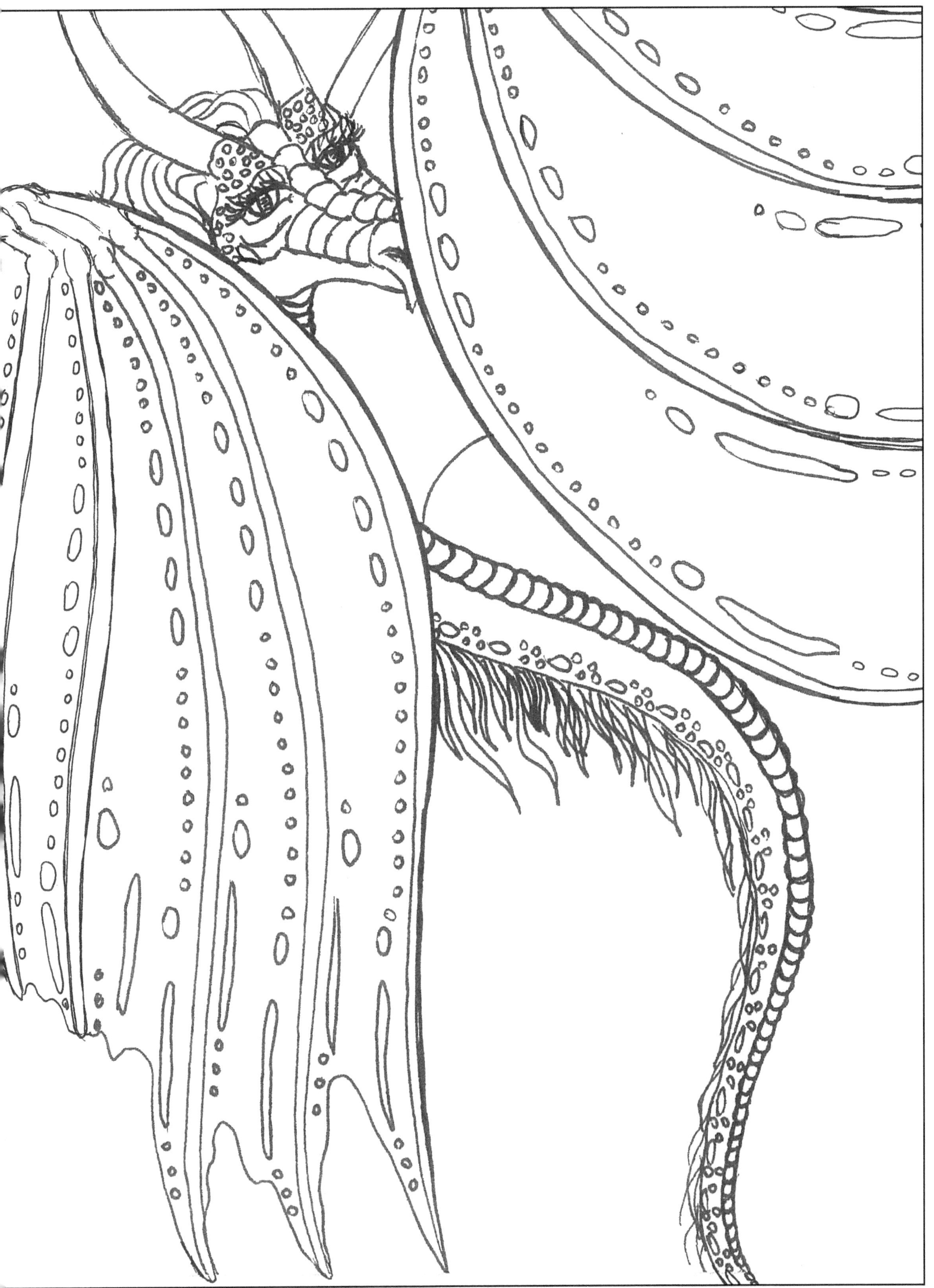

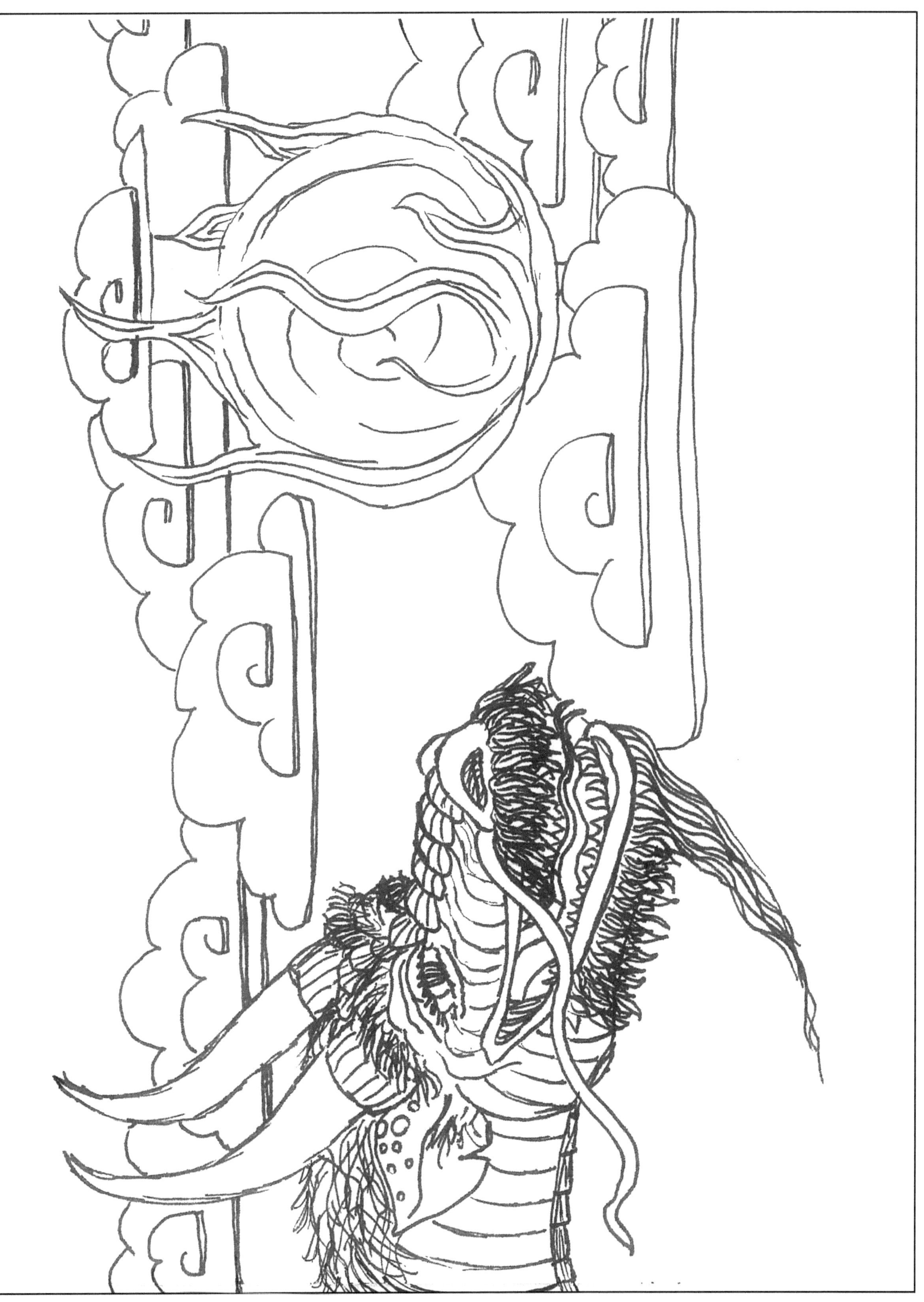

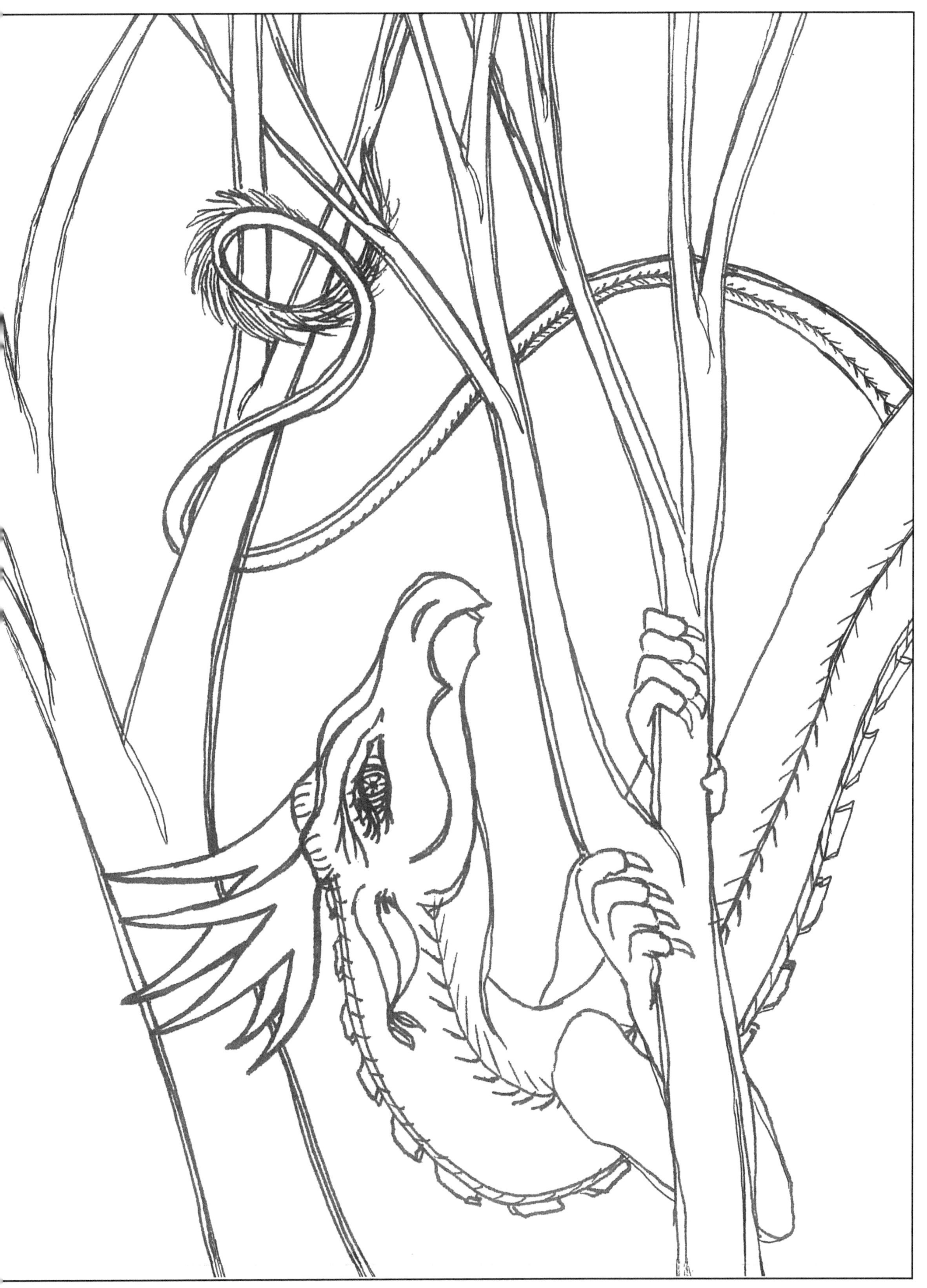

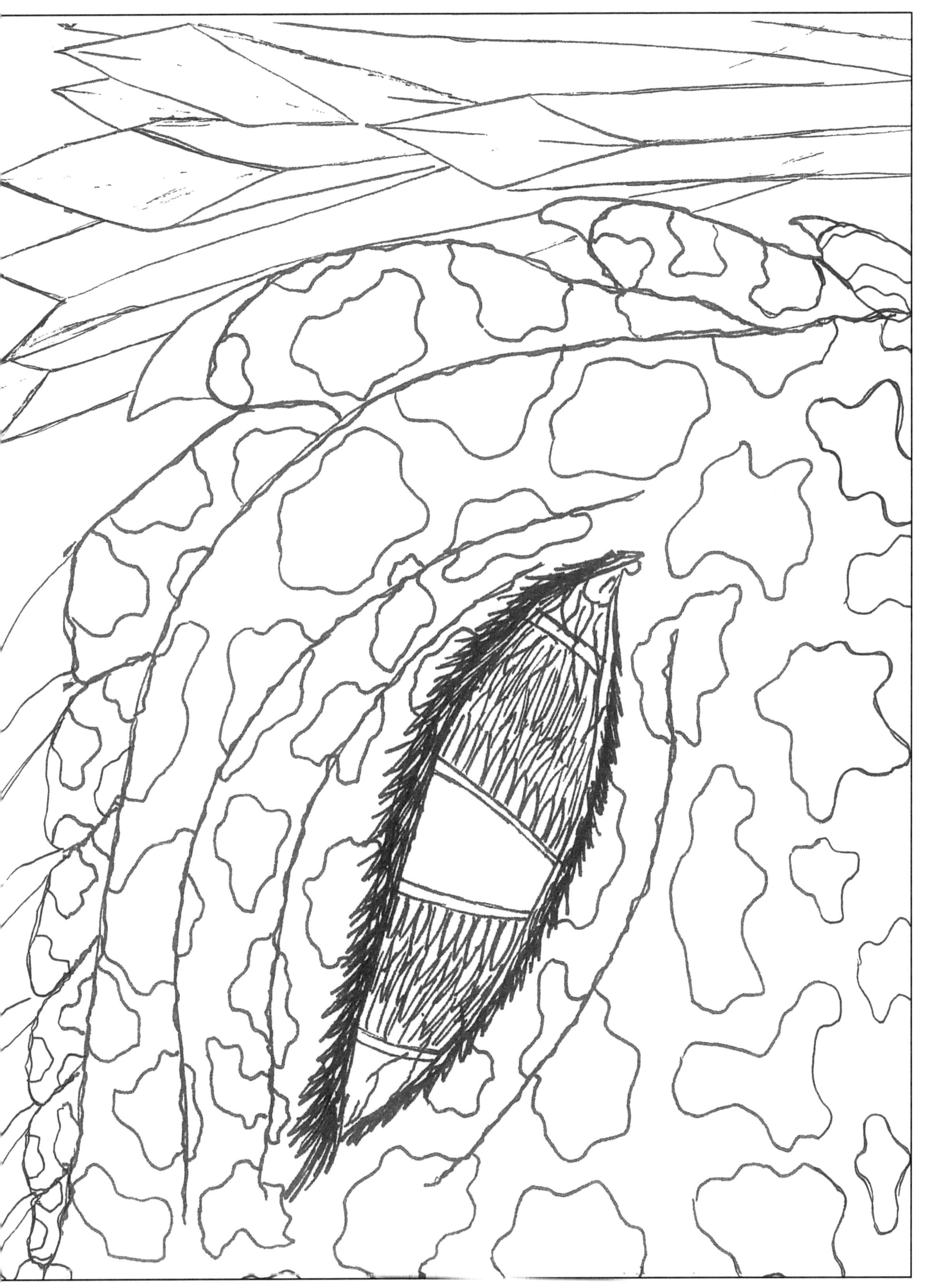

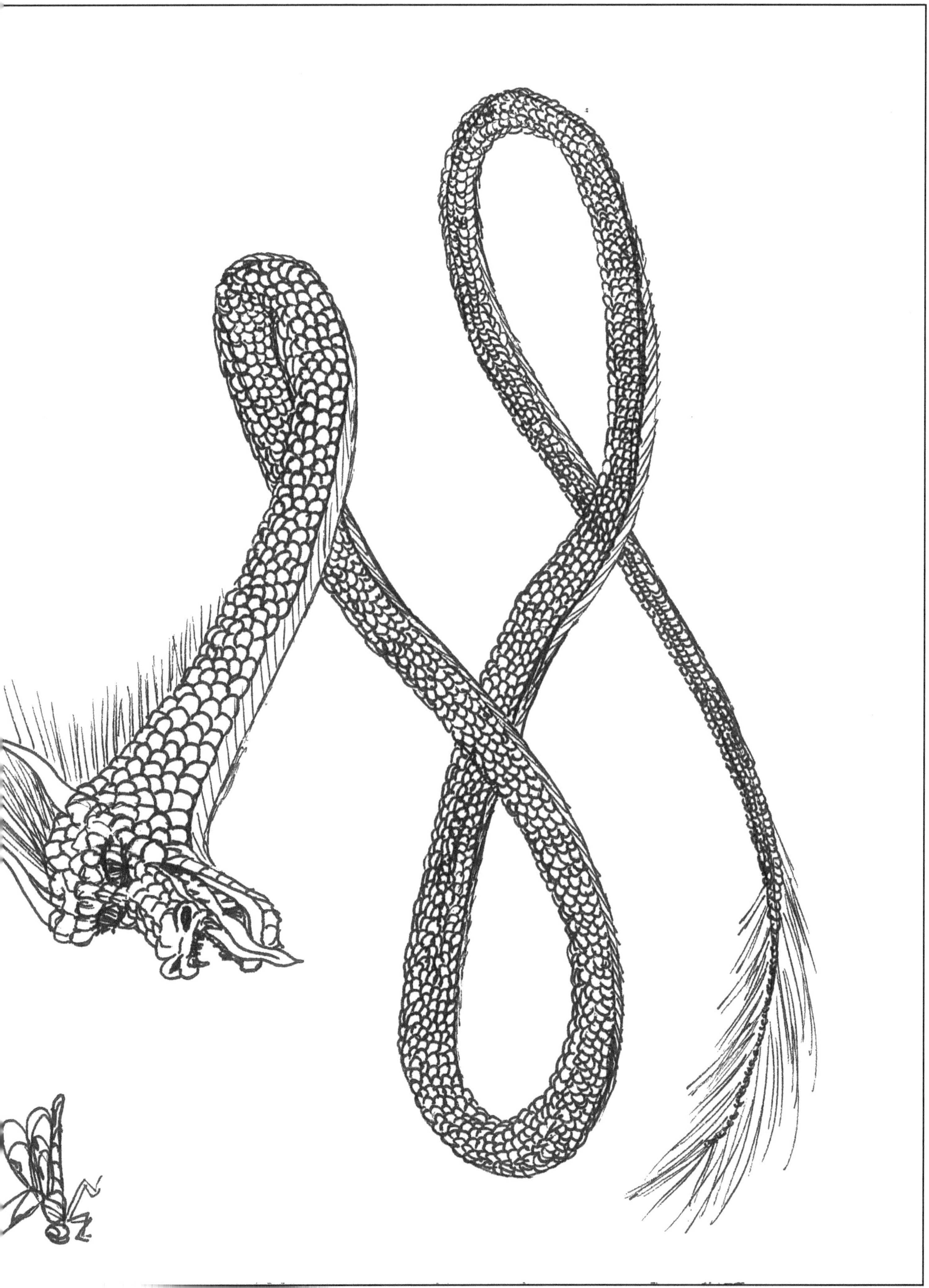

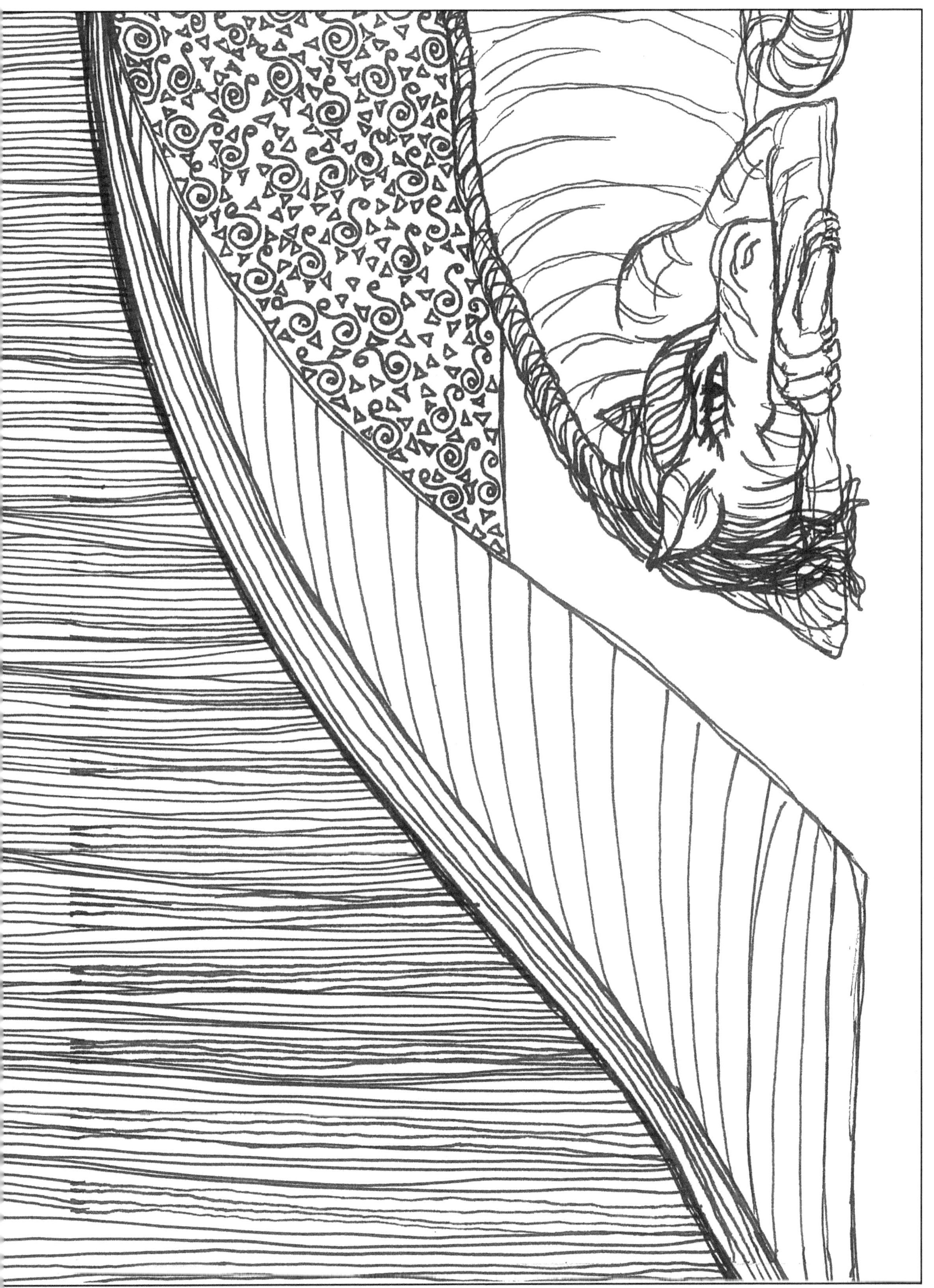

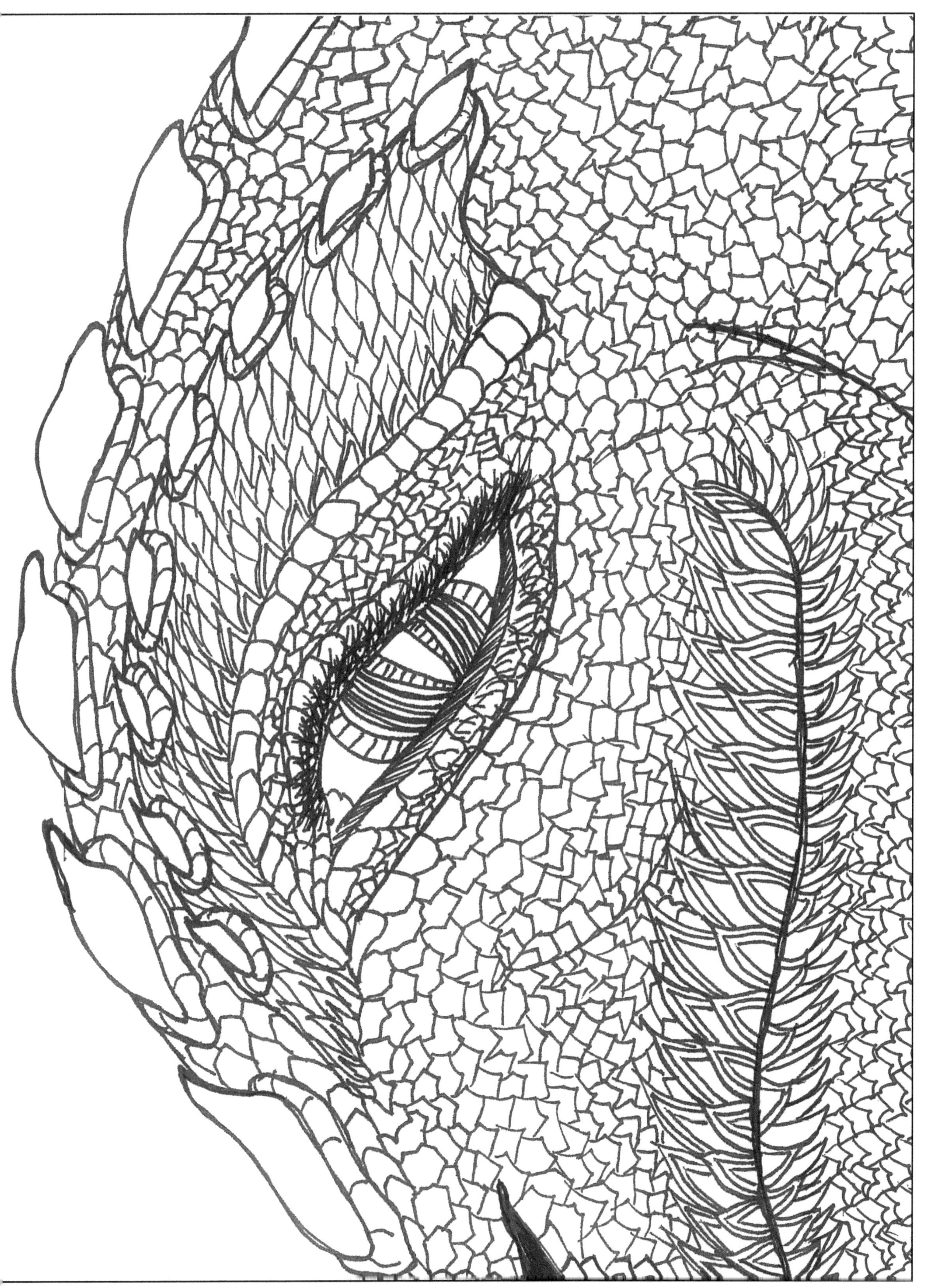

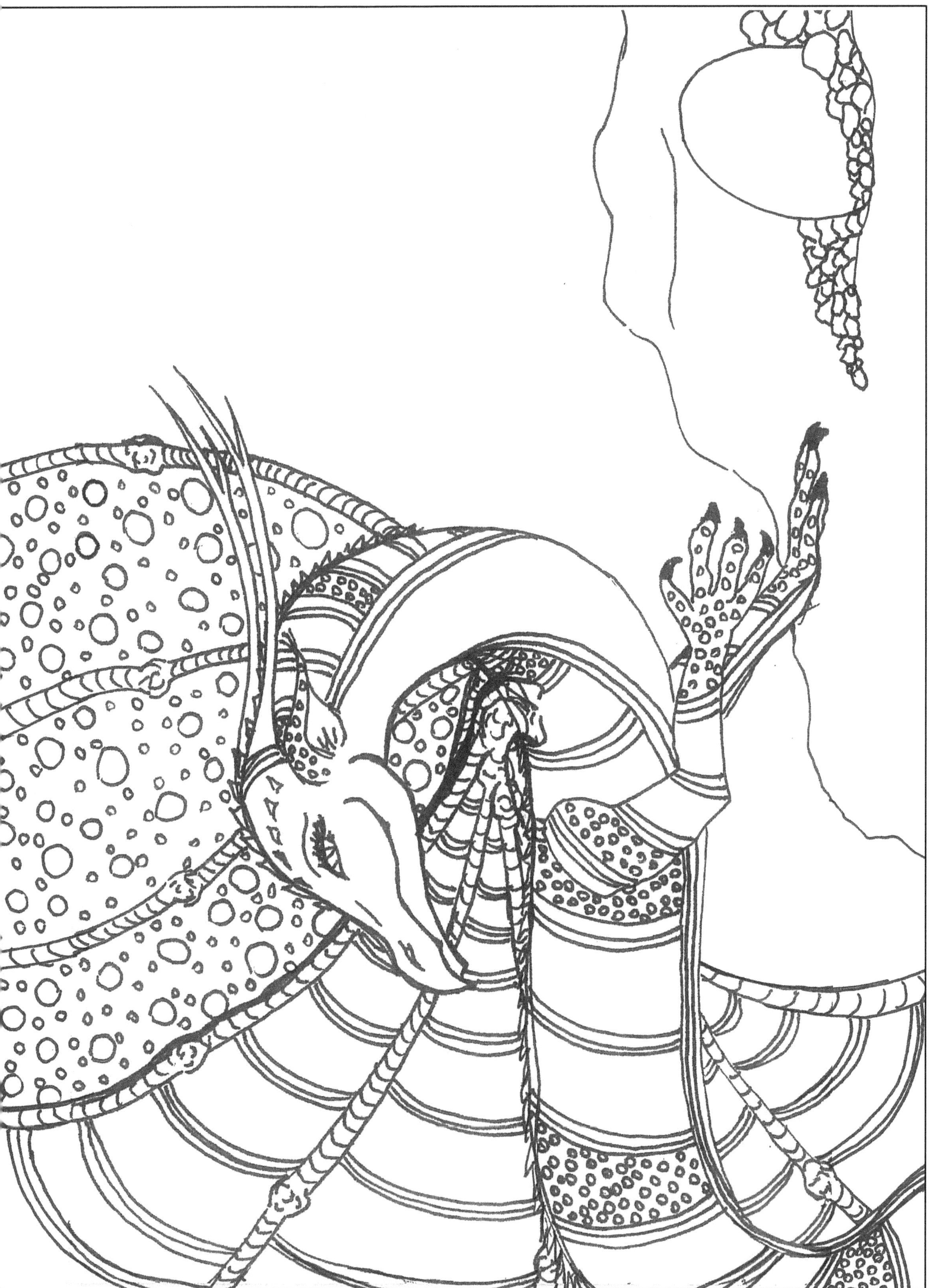

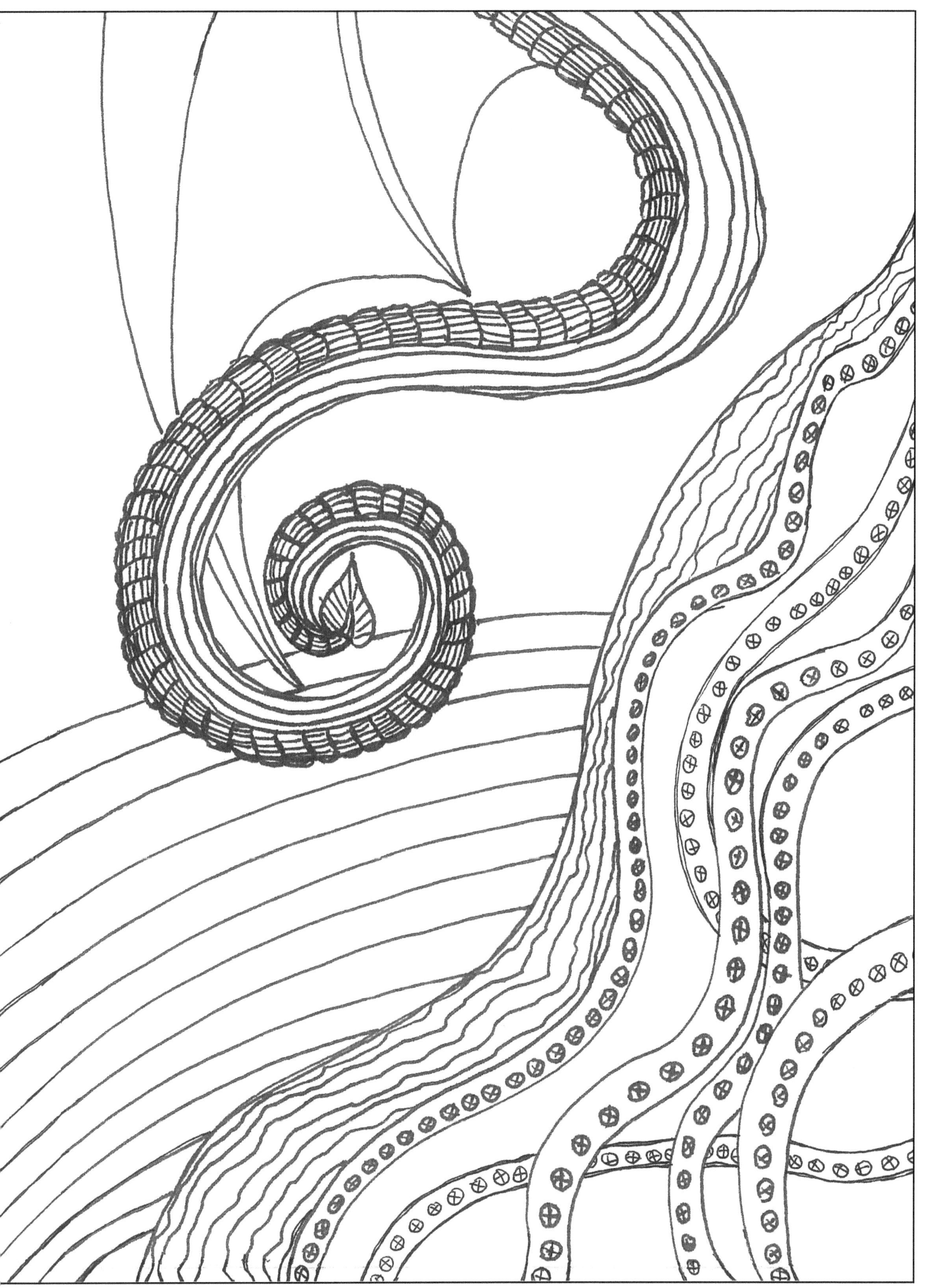

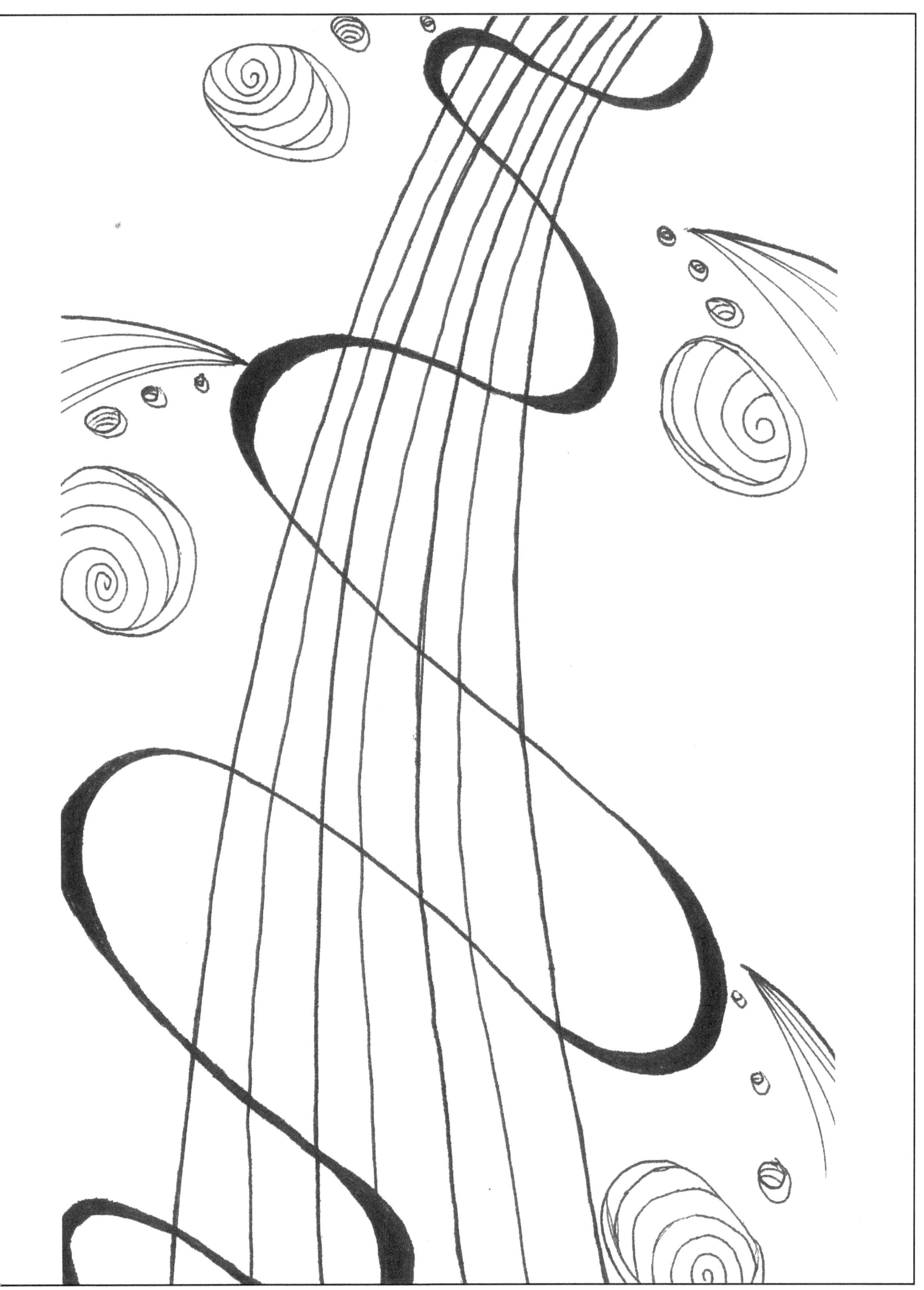